Stow Wengenroth's New England

STOW WENGENROTH'S
NEW ENGLAND

With Notes and Observations
by DAVID McCORD

INTRODUCTION BY SINCLAIR HITCHINGS

Barre Publishers · Barre, Massachusetts · 1969

Observer's Note

FOR PERMISSION to include certain copyright material in the contents of this book, I am indebted to the following individuals—in some cases to their estates, and in all cases to their publishers—as follows: To Howard Nemerov for three lines from his poem, "The Painter Dreaming in the Scholar's House," first printed by Boston College, copyright 1968 by Howard Nemerov; McGraw-Hill Book Co. and Helen Cruickshank, compiler, for a passage dated April 19 [1855] from *Thoreau on Birds*, copyright 1964 by Helen Cruickshank; the University of Massachusetts Press and Robert Francis for the poem "Seagulls," from *Come Out Into the Sun*, copyright by Robert Francis; Doubleday & Co., Inc., Faber & Faber, Ltd., and the estate of Theodore Roethke for eleven lines from his poem, "Meditation at Oyster River," copyright 1960 by Beatrice Roethke as Administratrix to the Estate, from *The Collected Poems of Theodore Roethke* (the poem originally appeared in *The New Yorker*); Random House, Inc., and the estate of Robinson Jeffers for the poem, "To the Stone-Cutters," from *The Selected Poetry of Robinson Jeffers*, copyright 1924 and renewed 1952 by Robinson Jeffers; Houghton Mifflin Co. and the estate of Rachel Carson for a brief passage from *The Edge of the Sea*, copyright 1955 by Rachel Carson; John Murray, London, the Beacon Press, and Freya Stark for a brief passage from *Perseus in the Wind*, published in England in 1948; Charles Scribner's Sons and John Hall Wheelock for the opening three stanzas of "Dear Men and Women," from *Dear Men and Women*, copyright 1966 by John Hall Wheelock; the Stephen Greene Press and Elizabeth Coatsworth for a paragraph from *Maine Memories*, copyright 1968 by Elizabeth Coatsworth; the *Atlantic Monthly* for a quatrain by David McCord; the Boston Public Library for a passage from my essay in *Art & Education*, copyright 1966 by the Boston Public Library; Little, Brown and Co. for ten lines from "Poet Always Next But One," in *The Old Bateau*, copyright 1941, 1950, 1951, 1952, 1953 by David McCord; Little, Brown and Co. for "The Door," and "Compass Song," from *Far and Few*, copyright 1925, 1929, 1931, 1941, 1949, 1952 by David McCord; Harcourt, Brace &

World, Inc., and the estate of T. S. Eliot for fifteen lines from "The Dry Salvages," in *Four Quartets*, copyright 1943 by T. S. Eliot.

For precise information on *strix davidi* (page 22) and a satisfactory identification (page 97) of the sapsucker of Jackson County, Oregon—the Rogue River country of my boyhood—I have to thank my friend, scholar and ornithologist William Cottrell. My owl stanza (page 22) is new.

Finally, I am indebted to Sinclair H. Hitchings for his important share in the genesis of this book, and for the introduction; to Stow Wengenroth, whose exquisite craftsmanship in a difficult art has made my far simpler task of commentary an unfailing pleasure; to Alden Johnson of Barre Publishers for believing in our venture and for reminding me, as work progressed, that publishing is in itself an art; to Ron Johnson and Gail Stewart for solving certain technical problems; and to Klaus Gemming of New Haven, whose design of this volume would seem to make the medium more than equal to the message.

D. T. W. McC.

Introduction

STOW WENGENROTH and David McCord share a love of the outdoors and a sense of the strength and loneliness of New England's rockbound landscape. Their book is a conversation, a comparing of experiences; our good luck, as readers, is to be able to listen in. The listening is both looking and reading, following the counterpoint between Wengenroth's pictures and McCord's words. In their dialogue, the particular can become a jumping-off point for a reach of thought and poetry into the universal, like the eye's reach toward a sea horizon and the mind's reach beyond it.

Both men are amateur naturalists, walkers, quiet watchers to whom the world of nature has shown some of its secrets. Both find nature the elemental, encompassing part of our world—one of those obvious and seemingly accepted facts which, in truth, have become almost meaningless to many city-dwellers today. Self-important humanity is wrecking its environment. We need to recover a sense of scale and setting; you will find both in the pages of this book.

Mr. Wengenroth and Mr. McCord are craftsmen, a word that already has a curiously antique sound. Wengenroth built his career on the same sense of the subtleties, mysteries, chemical facts and artistic possibilities of lithography that a generation of lithographers possessed in Paris a century and a half ago. To find someone to whom he might be compared, I have to go back to Nicolas-Toussaint Charlet (1792-1845), Auguste Raffet (1804-1860) or Eugène Isabey (1808-1868). As a prolific draughtsman on the lithographic stone, each had his special interests, subject-matter he returned to, as a composer may, in many variations, and each, as Wengenroth has done in our times, found a style of his own.

David McCord is a stylist in language, a new-minter of words as a poet should be. He is an essayist, too—another word that, like *craftsman*, suggests a vanishing breed of men. At least as important to what he says, in the pages of the present book, are his own skill in drawing and water-color, and his quiet pursuit of the collecting of art—prints, drawings, watercolors, oils, and, for sculpture, some fine woodcarving and a collection of owls in stone, pottery, porcelain and other materials, expressing in design and color the skills and concepts of people all over the world.

The Boston Public Library has been an ally—sometimes a working partner—in the making of *Stow Wengenroth's New England*, for all the lithographs reproduced in these pages come from the Library's collections. Years ago, Isabelle Knobloch, who had formed a complete collection of Wengenroth's prints, asked his advice about the best place for them after her death. He told her of the Library's print room and exhibition gallery, the Albert H. Wiggin Gallery, where a succession of print shows are held throughout the year. As a result, the prints by Wengenroth which she owned and enjoyed are now in Boston, and each year, through her thoughtfulness at the time she made her decision, Wengenroth's newest lithographs are added to the collection. She would be as pleased as we are to see prints from her collection reproduced in a book which brings together lithographer and poet in the surroundings they like best—the woods and towns and rugged coast and Atlantic horizons of New England.

SINCLAIR H. HITCHINGS
Keeper of Prints
Boston Public Library

8

Stow Wengenroth's New England

SUNLIGHT, WISCASSET

PICTURES in books once leafed through, like pictures on the walls of good museums in far-off cities, have a way of haunting us. We saw them hastily for reasons now forgotten; but some arresting passage in them flits across our vision when the mood is on us and we are ready for reminding. I remember and often think of a certain seascape by the British painter Arnesby Brown in the Tate Gallery, seen first and last now almost forty years ago. I have forgotten nearly everything about it save one single bar of cloud: "Yonder bar of cloud that sleeps on the horizon" is the way that Emerson helps me in my reach for it. I couldn't sketch its outline. I think it lay aslant. The color was warm. No matter: it fixed itself and the painter's name upon a small-used band in my retrieval system, the way the deepening burins of Sir Muirhead Bone and Norman Wilkinson have left me scattered accents out of etchings I can now not easily identify. Value of values was what made them memorable. Mood-matching is a very subtle business.

The viewer of these pages, if he savors and relates the truly relevant, will make his own anthology of little things that count. If "people are friends in spots," as Santayana says, so are pictures and people. When you find, as often you will find, in a museum catalogue the detail of a painting, tapestry or other work of art, you are looking at an area which critics surely praised; and certainly with certainty at what the compiler saw in microcosm with a skilled, selective eye. What this book may do to you in part—for black and white does not beguile with color—is to deepen your sense of selectivity. After the first or second impression of the whole, the eye comes to rest on what for you is the essential. Praise yourself as well as the artist *if and when* (a trinity that Fowler would eschew) you take it for your own—take it and keep it for some very special need.

OCCASIONALLY in antique shops along the New England littoral you may come across the stout old fine-spoked wheel of the trim bark *Alphadelta* or the *Nancy Belknap*, smooth and varnished as perhaps it never was when the second mate's big hands laid hold to come about. Or again you may share an elderly landlubber's sheer astonishment on finding such a wheel—though not of rich mahogany and teak—with an outer dowel-like rail of ash around it, joining all the end-notched spokes with the fit of a wagon tire. This is the wheel of a river boat, from Holland it may be, so added to for fast and easy spinning.

Man has a hanker in the end to make things easy. And easy in appearance is the drawing of some of the Ogunquit dunes that took the artist's fancy. You could almost do it yourself— and so could I—were it not for the flight of seven terns. They give the composition that *final* ease and grace of motion which the outer rim imparted to the old ship's wheel, just as the Wengenroth title gives it voice.

These terns are among the artist's most engaging and successful birds: speed, balance, contrast—four from underside, three from above. And note the utmost skill with which the third bird from the right is etched against the darkest scraggle of the pine and the whitest (zero) quality of sand. And perhaps you failed to notice the leading tern at all: not so aerial as numbers two and three, but still a needed accent *in* the air.

CRY OF THE TERNS

TREE AND ROCK: an old affinity in artists' eyes and on their sketch pads. How much of it we know from Japanese and Chinese scrolls, where trees seem often sprung from rocks themselves. Sprung, but almost always in a decorative pose. The study opposite, so pure in isolation and self contrast, tells me something of prevailing winds. It also tells me something of geology: shadows as distinct from lichens. It talks dead wood: hard, almost brittle dead. It wills me something (more important) in the legacy: the fierce tenacity of life.

Sermons in stones? Is ever self-injunction to survive more graphically revealed than by a wind-worn tree? Trilobite or amphioxus? Starfish? They do not show their struggle. Nor does the ant in amber. This solitary rock-bound tree proclaims it. No Landsturm, never summoned, gave protection. His roots may split the granite that long since provided shelter. His lance is better than his shield. We've seen a thousand trees; the twisted cedars of Carmel, Point Sur, in more elate design. Here is the simple toughness of New England: straight as the backbone will of Francis Parkman as he rode the western plains.

THE LANDMARK

WILLOWS AND WATER. Slaves to our cars today, we drive down roads where we remember the long line of willows uprooted in their prime just to make that extra right-hand lane where beepless VW's sneak by you after hiding in your blind spot. It is the rare back road today still double-lined with willows. Along Route 2, near where it crosses Thoreau's Concord River, they trim the weeping ones that overhang the westbound traffic so that they look like new-clipped sheep dogs out of Brobdingnag.

But here are willows in their separate glory: not yellow in the spring—though they are always that to me—but ancient and advanced in summer in the way they sort themselves in light and shadow. This is a favorite Wengenroth of mine for the way the artist handles the agenda on his plate. Is one thing out of order? Out of place? Not a single trailing strand of green, so far as I can tell.

CAPE ANN WILLOWS

WHY is so warm a picture of a house far from decay
so utterly lonely; the tall grass grown to the steps; not a bird,
not a gull in sight; those worn planks of the old porch aimed
so clearly at the vanishing point as in the saddest drawings
of Edward Lear? And yet it *is* warm—almost to the touch;
and doubly masterful for that white plane of purity above
the overhang which one dark window serves to magnify.
The sole eyes, which are yours, cannot escape the way that
two legs—which are yours as well—must walk. The tide
seems fairly high, else all one's spirit would be drained out
with it. And yet, for all of that, the warm diffusing sun
remains to make what we are looking at so memorable.

SEASON'S END

THE ILLUSION that we always look at pictures and that pictures never look at us is very strong. Yet portraits in which the eyes were painted to focus on the painter can give one the willies. And if they are the eyes of a woman—take another glance at the Mona Lisa—the effect is not at all what Goethe suggested at the close of *Faust:*

> *Das Ewig-Weibliche*
> *Zieht uns hinan.*

From this derives the rime old dodge of putting these thyroid lenses on a billboard, whereby I guarantee that they will spot you down the street and fix you with a swivel and hypnotic gaze until you are out of sight.

Of course, this common phenomenon is a useful way of reminding us that certain compositions in themselves may have the power to entrap the not too casual glance. "The Last Supper," according to Dali, has this power—at least it does for me. It is the partial secret—but the *partial* secret only—of the genre of *trompe-l'oeil*, where thumbtacks invite you to pull them out, or where you reach by reflex to save a fluttered paper from being blown off the canvas.

But I do not remember ever seeing a pen and ink drawing, an etching, lithograph, or wood engraving which possessed the camera eye as does this little masterpiece of persuasion. Far from wishing to enter these seeming empty or abandoned buildings, I am held a prisoner by some blinding headlight, searchlight, multipurpose torch, whatever it is. Too strong for the moon, too focused and too white to imply a nearby fire, what fascinates me in the planned result are all these details of reflection on the door, walls, chimneys, ladder-rungs, dried putty on the window panes, basket and barrel rims; yes, even on the grass.

And all in such compact small compass! Burchfield sometimes achieves this effect in a more sinister and haunting manner: trees like owls, stars dripping with light, flowers electrified as if they grew in some enchanted forest. But Burchfield worked in color. Here, more deeply to its purpose, displayed (as Melville says) with "reverential dexterity," is the color of night. And should you care to study values and consider a *Walpurgisnacht*, do what that artist does. Turn the book upside down. I do not wonder that I have seen this print in a dealer's window at a higher price than almost any other work by Mr. Wengenroth.

ONE OWL which I shall never see is *Strix davidi*, named for his collector, Père David. He is found in China, in the mountains of western Szechwan. David's owl, I call him; and he stands at the head of my Pallas Athena list. He is related to *Strix uralensis*, the Ural owl, widespread in the eastern palearctic. A pretty pair of words when written out, and a brace of lovely sounds: Ural Owl. Years ago in the Luxembourg in Paris I picked up a catalogue which I still treasure; a catalogue listing in three languages the works of the elegant sculptor François Pompon—elegant; and modern ahead of his time. The English for *chouette*, after the printer and proofreader had wrestled with it, came out *Orol*; the handwritten *w*, I suppose, having looked like *ro*. So *Ural Orol* is even better than Ural Owl. Say it over to yourself. How Edward Lear, with his *sparry in the pilderpips* alembic, would have smiled through his thick lenses. As for me:

> *Owls' eyes have little soul,*
> *of course: they see things whole;*
> > *white rats the French ones see*
> > *transfigure* la nuit;
> > > *Hibou*, mon vieux, that *one*
> > > *says* húlule—*quelque fun!*
> Húlule *means úlulate—*
> falsetto, *voicing fate.*
> > *Coots do it, and the loon,*
> > *ideally with a moon.*
> *Latin in latent state,*
> *Hibou húlules his mate*
> > *while* malheureux-x-x *go cats,*
> > *in Paris, having spats.*

THE SAGE

THIS snow-white drifting shudder from the farthest north must be a marvelous bird. I thought I saw one once in flight near Hingham, Massachusetts. I have looked for him on staddles—those circular low wooden pedestals for stacks of marsh grass still quite visible from littoral New England, I suppose, to New Brunswick's Tantramar. But not a one has ever sat for me. It was Ludlow Griscom, I am sure, who told me of the few who once made their bed in the tower of Memorial Hall at Harvard, and found their board with the rats on the dump at Watertown. I never saw them. All I know is, I prefer Lear's arctic owls to Audubon's—for composition and delineation—and prefer this one by Mr. Wengenroth to either. My preference is based not on a knowledge of ornithology which I do not possess, but on the pose and dignity of pose, a characteristic also of the owls in Tuttle's etchings.

It is odd to me that no one has written a book in novel form about the owl comparable to *Red Fox* by Sir Charles G. D. Roberts or to that genuine masterpiece by Henry Williamson called *Tarka the Otter*. Sally Carrighar or Farley Mowat would be the ones to do it now. Miss Carrighar for some years lived in Alaska and Mr. Mowat gave immortality to two owls (Wol was the name of one) in his hilarious yet lovable story of *The Dog Who Wouldn't Be*. Or why not Sterling North because of *Rascal?* Or Hal Borland, who has the knowledge and prose style and lives in good owl country? Meanwhile I am grateful for one triumph little known: *A Brown Owl* by H. M. Tomlinson.

Under his feather overcoat, the big owl or the small one is a scrawny kind of pretzel of a bird. Eyes, claws, and beak all terrify. His wings, "with sound-deadening filaments at the tips of the flight and contour feathers," are absolutely noiseless in their beat: no whicker of the flicker, whistling of the teal, or flapping of the crow. He was aeons ahead of Hollywood, and ladies with dark glasses nesting in their hair, by developing a third eyelid—nictitating membrane is its name—wherewith to cut the sun's glare or to feign to be asleep by day. His most enormous eyes are fairly fixed; they turn like bold binoculars precisely as he moves his head upon a neck much longer than his feathers would suggest. He can move it N to S, 180°, or all that panoramic vision would require. His facial disk, so marked in the common barn owl, resembles a portable tracking station; and the stirring of a mouse must therefore sound to him like echoes from a sunspot in eruption. Into his wide mouth go feathers, fur, and bones of captured prey. And after his stomach acids have considered and reported on them, up come the pellets of the residue, almost (it seems) as dry as dust.

SNOWY OWL

STREET LIGHTS and plastered snow, and a village touched by magic at the end of a great storm. This stroboscopic moment of such a night has the simplicity of an Edward Hopper water color (picket fence, porch shadow on the side of the second house); the frozen firefly eeriness of a Burchfield (those window-eyes of that same second house; the demon quality of branches to the right); and the tonal values in the Mansard roof contrast the warm house (right) with the cold house (left). Why is one warm and the other cold? I can't say. I simply know they are because the artist wants me to.

EIGHT P.M.

WHARF AT WELLFLEET

I SEEM TO REMEMBER, and don't wish to look it up for fear I am wrong, that in *The Rise of Silas Lapham*, Mr. William Dean Howells says that Boston's Back Bay, beginning near the middle 1850s, was filled in largely with oyster shells. Unlike Commonwealth Avenue west of the Public Garden, the rise of these fish houses still reveals just what they stand above.

It troubles my boyhood remembrance of raising chickens on Long Island that a ramp Down East (if such it is, off to the right) is called a chicken ladder. It has no cleats, which chicken ladders, concerned with toes the color of buttered popcorn, offer to the poultry traffic at intervals just equal to a leghorn pullet's stride. But then, I shall never understand the sea or those who go down to it in punts.

Note the treatment of light under the middle house. There is an air of lowtide desertion about this study which the single distant sloop appears to dramatize. It has no sails, it is not rigged, and no one is aboard; and yet we may take it for a definite symbol of life (very small) to balance the lifeless (very large). And it succeeds.

CERTAIN MEN, like certain mountains, slope by nature to the sea. If they are not actually on it, or do not make their living out of its abundance, they will choose to live within the sight and sound and smell of it, with kelp, sea lettuce, bladder wrack, knotted wrack, unitemized detritus and freak flotsam washing to within a dozen rods of their front doorsteps. Down East they often snug in close on arable low land to which they give the name "saltwater farm." Or else they cluster in some tiny village strung out along the one main street to front a wild and narrow harbor, where a big incisor had been pulled from the jaw of the land many millions of years ago; or so it would appear when you spread out a map.

How innocent, remote, and civil seems this present fragment of man's habitation by the sea. We have come across its people, surely, in *The Country of the Pointed Firs*. Down such a road as this the doctor and his not yet famous daughter, who had still to write her masterpiece, might once have driven. Kipling and Henry James both praised her; Willa Cather was her younger friend; and *My Antonia*— great novel that it is—owes a little something to Miss Sarah Orne Jewett. But even in our own time in such a peaceful village might occur (as did occur) the incident which the poet Elizabeth Coatsworth has described in her astute, attentive way in one short paragraph of her *Maine Memories*, published but one year before the page that you are reading went to press. It is all about one family's momentary ménage, the like of which two boys could gather only at the edge of the wild. The young seal, incidentally, was the gift of a fisherman whose dory it had followed home.

That morning the little seal had been taken in a wheelbarrow down to the cove half a block away for its day of swimming, but as usual it had grown hungry before it was called for again, and had flipper-flapped its way home along the concrete sidewalk, practically stopping traffic. I remember its fat baby face, its round eyes, and its whiskers which twisted in corkscrews. Bee Day was coaxing it away from the flower border with a fish while the two little foxes, with their pointed faces and big ears very large for their tiny bodies, dashed about through the tall grasses like excited demons. The puppy barked ecstatically, but it was the kitten which really played with the cubs, lying in wait for them, dashing out from ambush, to roll and scuffle with them on the warm earth. Seeing our amusement, the boys let out a big hare, which hopped about placidly, and then joined the sport by allowing the little foxes to chase it, and then chasing the cubs in turn, leaping over them in a great bound.

Such is the large tranquillity of this deephaven. There is more to the story, of course. But then, as Stephen Paget says of Nature: she

> Lives through all life, extends through all extent,
> Spreads undivided, operates unspent.

NEW ENGLAND VILLAGE

THESE TERNS, swift shadow-casters on the sand, are in before the gathering storm. No sun, no shadows this surf-breaking day. Their evolutions are too fast, too close to us, to phase us into their geometry. It takes the gulls for that; and I suspect the loftier wings of slower beat far off are gulls in traffic patterns of their own. Nor is it a day of thermals for gulls soaring. But gulls on the wing in the wind still have that slower grace I find enchanting, like the wayward flight of cabbage butterflies across a summer field. So the terns, arpeggiotic as a flute, give way unto or introduce with English horns the gull. Here is what Robert Francis wrote in "Seagulls"—an exercise exquisite in its poise. There is curving in the very *sound* of tercet, the stanza form in which these lines are written.

> *Between the under and the upper blue*
> *All day the seagulls climb and swerve and soar,*
> *Arc intersecting arc, curve over curve.*
>
> *And you may watch them weaving a long time*
> *And never see their pattern twice the same*
> *And never see their pattern once imperfect.*
>
> *Take any moment they are in the air.*
> *If you could change them, if you had the power,*
> *How would you place them other than they are?*
>
> *What we have labored all our lives to have*
> *And failed, these birds effortlessly achieve:*
> *Freedom that flows in form and still is free.*

IN FROM THE SEA

SEEING a flawless film of a real boss English cooper making a cask—a barrel to the layman—from the felling, quartering, and staving of the oak to the dowelling and fitting of the heads, renewed in some of us the love of working with fine wood. The grain and flavor of the carefully chosen tree seemed just as sharp on the screen as if the audience could touch and smell it. And we could sense the hot fire in the iron cresset while the half-bent staves were charred and heated.

Now see, on a smaller screen, how clear and unmistakable the look of this old splintered cedar. You can trace the shingly texture as the artist grains it for you; and in one place you can run your finger on a passage smooth and slippery as a piece of polished sandalwood. And what a hallmark is that cedary twist around the knots! As to the owl: how perfect, unobtrusive in his place, requiting values. Imagine him somewhere else? He relates just where he is: one silent witness that a master draftsman, like the master cooper, has the critic's eye for detail. That face, a split paraboloid for contemplating sound, is cunningly itself reflected in the fox-like one-eared owl-knot in the finely contoured wood beneath his belly. Intentional? Instinctive? What difference does it make?

LITTLE OWL

AIRPORTS have the sandglass fascination of the nervous second-hand that monitors a watch: the shadow of the Now moves thin and flickering across the sundial of Eternity. The savory sound of Joseph Conrad's "Landfalls and Departures" does not fit. Everything is urgent. Man is either in or out of the In and Out baskets: so much human freight to be handled, weighed, fed, hostess-hovered, and computered from one Main Street to another, day to darkness, rain to snow, ski pants to shorts. Harbors otherwise.

Time has stopped in this one. The voyage that is over, the one not yet on the log, are history and conjecture. Barnacles are up for scraping, hull for painting, gear for overhauling. Tide is the only certainty that must be met. A thousand planes will eat the miles in traffic patterns that this proud cargo vessel will pay out in foamy wake on her next sailing. This dockside, these old piles and wharves, seem dedicated to decay. But so is the floor of the forest, the weathered ledge of rock at timberline: true havens of another sort. One does not have to sail the sea to be becalmed.

Years ago I saw a schoolmate off from Maine's Wiscasset, bound for Labrador and a dangerous winter with a tribe of nomadic Indians on the move. He was an anthropologist and knew a lot about man's feud with time. He was in no hurry; never glanced at his watch. I look at this small harbor scene and think to myself: I would depart with a ripple, not with a roar.

GLOUCESTER DAYS

COAST OF MAINE

COLOR. Who says there is an absence of color in good black and white? One of the mysteries of the lithographer, etcher, and the man with chisel, pencil, pen, or charcoal is the *illusion* of color which he gives you— "the mystery and the air of interior beauty that accompanies a haunting poem." (I am quoting Charles Lewis Hind: *Adventures Among Pictures*.) Often the color is every-where: a kind of "inferred third harmonic," as a brilliant friend of my youth used to say of music. This for me is a color sense produced by subtle counterpoise of areas of different values. Sky, clouds, woods, beach, rocks, grass, houses all suggest the colors we half *think* that we imagine.

The *real* imagination went into the lithograph in this case because the artist could not leave it out. For example, there is sunlight on the whitewash, and in its concentrate we feel instinctive warmth. So the whole composition takes on warmth, the way that Whistler's decimal lights in "Waterloo Bridge" relieve the basic grey not quite surrendered to the dark. And as to that: for twenty years I have admired a black-and-white photograph of an eerie Addams-like house and owl-like pine trees which Charles E. Burchfield gave me. His original watercolor I have never seen; but that curious electric, epigenic quality in the best of his great work creates a color illusion even in monotonic reproduction.

Of course there is—there must be—now and then a sense of color blindness in the viewer when imagination is too low in key. The Indians discovered that in absolute pitch darkness breathing rapidly will give the human eye some quality of owl-sight. So the artist cunningly contrives his shades of black as if indeed Payne's grey and Davy's grey, both slightly warmed above their neutral state, were here at work. In wood engravings this effect for me is even more apparent. The rolling bare-topped hills in Thomas W. Nason's later studies of Vermont produce a close approxi-mation of bleached grass. Our case in point is color values in the sea and sky as well as in the lighthouse.

IT IS THE DENSITY of this dark wood beyond the sunlit space or entrance where we stand that makes it so attractive and mysterious. The fallen tree has been down far too long to make one feel at home upon a well-worn trail. This is, by rapid estimate of size, a virgin forest; doubtless a most silent one, with nothing more to listen to than vagrant air astir among the needles, or the scolding of a squirrel, resentful of our bold intrusion.

Now the artist can imply great silence just so long as he has mastery over mood. And mood is what this flawless wood interior creates. I wish to be there for the clean green smell of pine and nothing else. A bird or animal, I think, artistically would *rouse* resentment. Nor could I ask that where the sunlight does not fall and all is black, our sight should leave the magic circle for a glimpse of field or mountain.

Yet mood, when so intense, awakes the memory; and I recall a time and place when such a stand of trees would lead me to the sound of running water: the downhill dactyl voice immortal to the fisherman. I see and hear, so gratefully, my youth across the silence of this nooning hour: the time, of course, reported by a dozen dead-branch sundials. I sense the murmur of a distant stream that nothing on this Eden earth surpasses for delight.

> *By ledge of cedar root and stone*
> *I hear the hidden bird unflown,*
> *Cathedral in his tree above*
> *The level of my river-love.*

COOL FOREST

IT IS—is it not?—impossible to look on these white, empty pews unmindful of the angle of vision as being that of a man's two eyes, if he should kneel in prayer and suddenly raise his head. It is the view precisely, save for the scattered congregation, I remember as a boy when I stood, my round eyes popping over the back of what was in front of me, to observe it as a chess board covered with bare-headed knights and kings, and queens in Easter bonnets.

But in this village church of Castine, Maine, though I can guess the period, denomination, and possibly parishioners, I cannot hear the prayers of hope, doubt, fear, and anguish; of thanksgiving and remorse, word within Word; the summoning bell for times of joy and grief. Tongues in the trees? Look through the windows.

Consider, finally, the words of a third Long Islander (Mr. Wengenroth is one; I was once the second) in these three opening stanzas of "Dear Men and Women," by John Hall Wheelock, dedicated to the memory of Van Wyck Brooks.

They are offered, simply, with those commas in their place, as a benediction to simplicity. Is there a living poet under the Psalmist's three-score-ten who could or would have written these three stanzas? I think not. Four points to the compass: architect, carpenter, artist, poet.

In the quiet before cockcrow when the cricket's
Mandolin falters, when the light of the past
Falling from the high stars yet haunts the earth
And the east quickens, I think of those I love—
Dear men and women no longer with us.

And not in grief or regret merely but rather
With a love that is almost joy I think of them,
Of whom I am part, as they of me, and through whom
I am made more wholly one with the pain and the glory,
The heartbreak at the heart of things.

I have learned it from them at last, who am now grown old
A happy man, that the nature of things is tragic
And meaningful beyond words, that to have lived
Even if once only, once and no more,
Will have been—oh, how truly—worth it.

MEETING HOUSE

VIEWING this baitsmell motley—*sursum corda!*—of bunged barrels, fishnet, boxes, lobster pots, pot buoys, hoist, pulley, rope, and other gatherabilia—my word, that, not Joyce's—reminds me of a well-turned, thawed-out sentence in *Finnegans Wake*. Also, that Joyce would have written *lobsterspots;* and how should I know if he didn't? I have spent by count but eighty beguiling hours on his foggy stardust journal writ in "cholk and murble in lonestime." The quote that I was reaching for (as out of the Davy dark of Dylan Thomas) is suggestive or ingestive of the lobster on the ocean's floor, "making sharpshape his inscissors on some first choice sweets fished out of the muck." Joyce sharpshaped his inscissors on the apostrophe in *Finnegans*. Two other famous titles deal with places (1) real and (2) imaginary, and likewise do not show the possessive: *Gallions Reach* by H. M. Tomlinson, and *Howards End* by E. M. Forster. There may be others equally well known, but I am inclined to think not. Bunyan had his seventeenth-century chance to pioneer with *Pilgrim's Progress,* but he missed it.

Beyond its tactile and flavorsome quality, what I like about this lithograph is the subtle, unobtrusive treatment of the water and reflections in the cove.

WHEN WE LOOK beyond the stranded boats we
think of the beach; and to think of the beach, thoughts
flock together like a run of sanderlings, their tiny legs
criss-crossing in a blur as they follow the frothy lip of thin
retreating waves "like a clockwork toy." The artist, with a
scene like this, does not have to animate. The mind of the
beholder will do that easily for him. It seems to me that we
have in this composition of serenity a perfect setting for
eleven of the final fourteen lines of Theodore Roethke's
quiet three-score-ten-line "Meditation at Oyster River":

> *Now, in this waning of light,*
> *I rock with the motion of morning;*
> *In the cradle of all that is,*
> *I'm lulled into half sleep*
> *By the lapping of waves,*
> *The cries of the sandpiper.*
>
> *Water's my will and my way,*
> *And the spirit runs, intermittently,*
> *In and out of the small waves,*
> *Runs with the intrepid shore birds—*
> *How graceful the small before danger!*

QUIET DAY

EUCLID alone has looked on Beauty bare"? One dares to say that when Millay set down this now familiar line, identified in feeling and idea with Wordsworth's "marble index" of Newtonian mind, she was thinking of mathematicians and of architects as well. Euclid was something of both, was he not? Nor must the astronomers be omitted, since their stellar search from little igloos on the hill and mountain tops has always called upon the largest slates and blackboards and the whitest chalk.

Well, here is an exercise in angles and diagonals; in planes and surfaces, circles and parabolas; in bridge mechanics, stress and strain; in light and optics, absorption and reflection. Everything in balance: transparency, opacity, wood and stone, metal and glass, design and purpose.

Cold? So the stars in the void are cold. Lonely? So is the eternal watchfulness of man. "Every word was once a poem," says Emerson; and three pages later, in the same still famous essay, he adds with much more relevance: "Language is fossil poetry." If the artist had caught but one or two of these self-evident truths—and he has caught so many—this would still remain a little monument of grace and style: a beacon quite apart from its intrinsic and explicit argument in favor of poetics in the absolute geometry.

TOWER DOOR

OF ALL OUR BIRDS that visit window feeders in America, the chickadee is probably the most exciting. Only the weasel can compare with him for speed. If you have ever watched a weasel in captivity enter the hole in his sleeping box and appear to be looking out of it all in one motion, you have seen the perfect balance and control of this enchanting member of the titmouse tribe. Of course the humming bird is swifter far; but *his* astounding acrobatics are entirely aerial. Besides, he is not dressed to take his workout on the parallel bars.

Think of the different and visibly gymnastic chickadees in Frank W. Benson's water colors. Mr. Wengenroth through sheer repose has chosen to convey the *sense* of action—of kinetic action—in these admired, companionable entertainers. And unrelatedly, has anyone recorded what the chickadee is saying in Morse international (continental) code? He says CHICKA (dash dot) DEE DEE DEE (dash dash dash) which is NO in English.

THREE OF A KIND

SHADOW OF THE ELM

Do YOU REMEMBER at the end of John Galsworthy's *Indian Summer of a Forsyte* those last words closing in as death is closing in on Jolyon?

Summer—summer—summer!
The soundless footsteps on the grass!

They come back to me now: unsummoned nine from limbo. I didn't have to look them up. They are the proper words, I think, to measure what old houses and old lawns can tell us of the generations of men long gone and not yet come. Which is what this sun-and-shadow study is about.

Xenogenesis, you may well argue, would account for this engaging study of three marionettes positioned in a book that shows no more than two or three examples of the human race. But the originals are the bright and tidy work of Mrs. Wengenroth (Edith Flack Ackley) and I look upon them with affection as a trio lurking there perhaps behind a door—a well known door which I once wrote about in terms of childhood.

Why is there more
behind a door
than there is
before:
Kings,
things
in store:
faces,
places
to explore:
The marvelous shore,
the rolling floor,
the green man
by the sycamore?

MARIONETTES

THOREAU in *Walden* speaks of "life pasturing freely where we never wander." How many countless times have each of us looked wistfully on meadows, fields, small valleys, great plains, intervals and intervales, gulfs, notches, gaps, low bottom land, clear maple groves, pine woods, birch clusters, swamps, green labyrinths of juniper, green pastures, daisy runs, dunes back of beaches, and wished for youth we do not still possess, for time we cannot spare, to wander just like Thoreau, Jefferies, Muir, Bolles, Brewster, Frost, and Edward Thomas. Hundreds of these thousand vistas opened to us from the train or car, perhaps from old cross-country trolleys—best of all man's minor links between a town and village. Some we saw and still see round accustomed bends, up over special hills; and yet we rarely pause. Why do we not?

Such is the invitation that the artist gives us; but he gives it with assurance that we shall not suffer through reality denied. We look where he has been, see what he tells us, usually have small notion beyond place names where we are. His moment of his own big venture lies before us, everlasting in his then and where. We may be reminded or caught up by some remembrance, but not by sheer frustration. What is told us we retell ourselves.

But perhaps the greatest pleasure which a landscape black and white can give us is the chance (as I have said elsewhere) to focus on some minor detail—tree trunk, branch, log, broken sky, such mystery in leaf or grass which wind, rain, snow, or season cannot alter, and to which we may return at will.

SANCTUARY

LIGHT AND SHADE are the essential quanta with which the western artist deals; unless one, say Matisse, is working in pure line. Light and shade in every medium: oil, watercolor, gouache, pastel, charcoal, pencil drawing, etching, wood engraving, aquatint, and lithograph demand a fine gradation of the two in subtlety of line reflection, undertone, and so on.

But now and then, especially with etchers, lithographers, and wood engravers, and lately with what I call the astigmatic school, whose members bend and flex their squares and rounds of black and white in fascinating, fluid patterns, we confront the dual world of absolutes. Look through the work of Manet (Raven), Seurat (Sunday on Grande Jatte Island), Redon (The Day), Braque (Milarepa), Munch (The Kiss), Nolde (The Prophet), Kandinsky (Abstraction), Feininger (Lehnstadt), Vallotton (The Flute), Burchfield (The East Wind), Rockwell Kent (illustrations for *Moby Dick*), Sheeler (Interior with Stove), Marc Simont (illustrations for Thurber's *The 13 Clocks*), for examples of sheer solids staring into white. Mr. Wengenroth is no exception. He can balance black and white in massive moments. There is a coldness in all this, of course; a shuddering coldness. But it fits the wild New England shore in this case quite as well as in the hands of others it translates for us bleak Labrador or Greenland or the Arctic Circle.

Above all, black and white in big block opposites for balance has great power. Anyone familiar with the modern *Moby Dick*, for which the pen and brush of Rockwell Kent were dipped into the void of night itself, will not forget first looking on them spellbound, page by page. As illustrations, they are *not* monotonous. As independents, strung together in one volume such as this, they would be. And so this early Wengenroth, somewhat in isolation, for effect. Likewise for power. Furthermore, it pleases me afresh today since Howard Nemerov, in a recent poem about a very different artist, has given me the words I could not lay my hands on:

> It is a language for the oldest spells
> About how some thoughts rose into the mind
> While others, stranger still, sleep in the world.

BLACK CAPE

HOW QUICKLY do the eyes of man accommodate the scale and size of what he looks at to reality, if what he looks at is not real but represented. We watch our television, not for Lilliputian figures, cutting down ourselves to size; we sit before the movie screen, not feeling we are of the kingdom of huge Brobdingnag, but cutting all these giants to the size of *homo sapiens—homo fictus* though they be. We do the same with pictures on the wall or in a book. I do not guess the lichens on these rocks as on a scale of x square inches to one. They are there for my inspection if I could walk where Mr. Wengenroth has been before me. He has given us a glimpse of rocks and conifers in all their secret sway within the heart of some deep wood: a very skillful balance of the horizontal, perpendicular, and circular.

SAND DUNES have the privilege of a double life: the life of the sea and the life of the land; but of each of them only to a certain measure. Yet it is really the quintet of those great agents of the sky—wind, rain, ice, sun, and snow, that is—which shape and reshape, add to, subtract from, and position them.

Dunes are always on the move, appear and disappear in geologic time, but show their faculty of animation even in our own. Unusual or equinoctial tides, neap tides more sparingly, may level them in part: but the checkerboard hands which play them, dune for dune, against each other, are and ever were the shifts of wind, erosion under rain, ice, snow, and baking in the oven of hot noon. I can only guess the chemistry of these. All I know, as a one-time walker and sometime painter of dunes, is that their change continues more perceptibly than one would imagine. A handful of sand, I once observed, is an anthology of the universe. The cleanest handful, surely, would be found in what we see before us.

WINDY DUNES

THE PRESENT PASSION of the status-seeker seems to be in part for private swimming pools. If one has ever spent the fraction of a dry mercurial day at real dead center—say in Hastings, Nebraska—it is easy to see that a backyard pool would be a blessing. But to find them staggered on the seaside terraces is much too much like warming the hands at a bonfire in hell.

Here is a Rockport seaside pool for other purposes. The least of these, perhaps, is a walk around the edge. A better one for many is the chance to dangle one's feet over the edge and fish for cunners. Such walls—sea walls—of granite, matched and roughly mitred from the quarry, lend a quarry-look to what remains. Why travel to Egypt to see the pyramids or conjure up an androsphinx? Better to contemplate an earthquake toppling the Colossus of Rhodes, and do it here in retrospect beside the sea which man has tamed to his use: a peaceful bastion in all but the filthiest weather, behind which he may harbor his small craft as though some Gulliver had pulled them in by strings from Blefuscu to Lilliput.

OLD HARBOR

PERHAPS I go to the wrong museums; but now and then the carpenter, mechanic, handyman, lathe-turner, and electrical experimenter in me, as they were until I was fifteen, nudge me with the notion that not much of art today, save what the sculptors salvage from their secret pact with the junk dealers, is devoted to the delights of machinery. Dali bends a watch; girders spread and angle through abstractions; but the artist seldom comes to grips with dynamos and cracking plants, blast furnaces, those too giraffe-like mobile cranes—and this is a time of cranes and hoists and pile-drivers; with Diesels and nuclear plants, with laboratories, with the bowels of a ship. Kipling and Wells did; and E. M. Forster in "The Machine Stops." And poets from Whitman to Spender (as Honegger's *Pacific 231* in music) have extolled the locomotive. "Pulse of the continent" were Whitman's words. And, *pari passu*, the artist has accomplished something here akin in draftsmanship to Louis Untermeyer's matchless summary of Walt: "Employing words, he harnessed elements." Less dangerous, one might add, than employing equations.

This Rockport foundry, as a small-scale Piranesi, pleases by its composition: spare, but purposeful; simple, yet functional; idle, though not static with disuse. Here is no shed of porpoise oil for jewelers. Something big is afoot; big as the quarries not far distant. The one or two spare parts in sight are fit for unseen giants of horsepower. Atlas, in a moment, may hulk himself right through the doorway.

OVER the grass his wind will soon be blowing,
Over the sea his petrel shall come flying,
Over the range his cumulus be sailing,
Over the field his hound shall follow running;
Over the roof his smoke will lift, and rising
Over the wall his snow will drift, devising
Over the road his scroll and scrawl of snowing;
Over the trail his eye shall show its cunning,
Over the coast his fog will gather.
                                        Crying
Over the land, his word shall be unfailing.

MAINE FOG

UNLESS WE HONOR our commitment to this earth we shall not feel with poets, painters, sculptors, architects, typographers; with potters, stonecutters, wood-workers, craftsmen, and designers—with musicians even, though we have no tactile margin on that one great glancing art; nor shall we sense that in the things they do in smaller measure is reflected—though the artist be the last to tell you—something of the great design. This pantheistic premise does not mean that poets should be Wordsworth, painters pure Corot, engravers Bewick; or that buildings make Pueblos of us all. Only a fool would say that most great artists are in love with nature. Many are not and never were. Many despise in truth or in the dark the very noun. Picasso does not meet me on the beach, Chagall on mountain tops, Kandinsky in Omaha, Dufy (in spite of his brave woodcut "Fishing") on a trout stream. That is not the point. Even less the point that Picasso says "Through art we express our conception of what nature is not." The point is that dynamics, symmetry, suspensions, chords and monotones, surrealism and pop art; the last least curve or dot or butchered polygon or fractured rhythm; the break-up principle in such as Klee, the checkerboard of Euclid's traffickers in blacks and whites—all this, all these, all those, the astronomers, the physicists in solid state, marine biologists, conchologists, coleopterists, stress-testing metallurgists, and such microminded stroboscopic people in the lab have seen unfold. Ask the speleologist; ask the ranger in his wind-eroded Utah. Examine one Mount Palomar photograph of the great nebula in Andromeda. Examine crystals under fluorescent lights.

If anyone considers this statement a stretch of overheated imagination, let him look up *Natural History* for December, 1968, pp. 40-41, for extraordinary examples in color of (a) sand inclusions in azurite (startling modern sculpture); (b) two memorable landscape paintings created by "fine-grained minerals whose patterns are caused by impurities trapped during formation." The first is of rolling hills with hardwood trees in silhouette (a polished sample of jasper from Oregon); the second an unbelievable vignette of sun behind conifers (sedimentary agate from Arizona). This casual evidence, incidentally, has come to light almost two years after the paragraph above was written.

Form is everything; but form is never really new. Nature always got there just ahead of us. Only the use of form, the symphony of form, form formulating form, is new. A morning's walk out in the sun some unexpected country day will fit the least Thoreauvian among us to enter any gallery or museum. For what? For anything from Manet to Miró; from Homer to John Marin. For something old and proven; something wild, incredible. For all the snowflake fancy filigree and resignation of this tall, period gingerbread against a mackerel sky.

VICTORIAN ERA

IN THIS FESTOON of buoys, surely, the medium
is the message. Recall a hundred of them floating somewhere
just offshore in gay designs and colors, and there speaks
the branding iron of the sea atilt to every tide. The sight of
them at anchor in a sober groundswell under the lee of some
great overhang or ledge of rock says simply: lobster pots.
Tourists from the central states and out across the plains
regard them with a fascination; and they turn up manifold
among the best glass paperweights, old bottles, duck decoys,
and buttons in antique shops down along the eastern coast.
In the sea they dance and live the life of lively marionettes.
But here they hang, till bait and boat and season are in phase,
like Christmas decorations and bright tinsel in an outdoor
attic, unled-to by a flight of stairs.

LOBSTER BUOYS

HOW SKILLFUL is this minor composition: its arcane strength in one octagonal at top, genius in the single opaque pane, a delicacy that only Andrew Wyeth equals in the gathering of curtains at the right. How well the chimney is requited by the darker window-sash and by the shrub to one side just below it. A man will sometimes draw the way we bring bird glasses into focus: one seems to *see* things moving into place, into their ultimate relation; "the fidgets of remembrance," as Wallace Stevens said, all suddenly assembled.

WINDOW IN WISCASSET

INTERESTING beyond the lighthouse and the structural quality of this particular in-back scene—at least for me and my untutored eye for all geology—is the slate-like vertical of these upended slabs of rock: as though the vise and not "the weave of the world" had clamped a pile of headstones all together, even to their rounded tops. That line which I have quoted is not in the little poem— one of the best known poems—of Robinson Jeffers which follows. He wrote it in another connection. Stones, black cypresses, granitic mountains, and the fathomless sea—I am paraphrasing Louis Untermeyer—were rather close to him and his dark outlook on the world. So let him speak:

Stone-cutters fighting time with marble, you foredefeated
Challengers of oblivion,
Eat cynical earnings, knowing rock splits, records fall down,
The square-limbed Roman letters
Scale in the thaws, wear in the rain. The poet as well
Builds his monument mockingly;
For man will be blotted out, the blithe earth die, the brave sun
Die blind, his heart blackening:
Yet stones have stood for a thousand years, and pained thoughts
*   found*
The honey of peace in old poems.

ABANDONED LIGHT

THE BUFFLEHEAD (*Bucephala albeola*) has several colloquial names: Butterball, Spirit Duck, Spirit Dipper, and Woolhead, according to Helen Cruickshank, though Butterball is the only one familiar to me. Not much larger than the little teals, Buffleheads will nest in "holes deserted by flickers or other woodpeckers," says Mrs. Cruickshank, but do no nesting in New England.

Well as I thought I knew Thoreau, I am indebted to this intelligent naturalist and editor of *Thoreau on Birds* for isolating the following extract of April 19 [1855] from Thoreau's *Journal*. The cars to which Thoreau refers, need we be reminded? were neither Hupmobiles nor Franklins, but the cars of the Fitchburg Railroad; the same to which, some decades later, Kipling paid his respects with the once familiar warning to all and sundry—all and cindery: "Change here for Winchester, Ashuelot, Nashua, Keene, and stations on the *Fitch*burg Road!" Or don't you remember the first of the twelve *Just So Stories*, echoing Vermont? "From Heywood's Peak," said Thoreau—

From Heywood's Peak I thought I saw the head of a loon in the pond, thirty-five or forty rods distant. Bringing my glass to bear, it seemed sunk very low in the water,—all the neck concealed,—but I could not tell which end was the bill. At length I discovered that it was the whole body of a little duck, asleep with its head in its back, exactly in the middle of the pond. It had a moderate-sized black head and neck, a white breast, and *seemed* dark-brown above, with a white spot on the side of the head, not reaching to the outside, from base of mandibles, and another, perhaps, at the end of the wing, with some black there. It sat drifting round a little, but with ever its breast toward the wind, and from time to time it raised its head and looked round to see if it were safe. I think it was the smallest duck I ever saw. Floating buoyantly asleep on the middle of Walden Pond. Was it not a female of the buffle-headed or spirit duck? I believed the wings looked blacker when it flew, with some white beneath. It floated like a little casket, and at first I doubted a good while if it possessed life, until I saw it raise its head and look around. It had chosen a place for its nap exactly equidistant between the two shores there, and, with its breast to the wind, swung round only as much as a vessel held by its anchors in the stream. At length the cars scared it.

BUFFLEHEAD

A BIT OF MOLD," said Victor Hugo, "is a pleiad of flowers; a nebula is an anthill of stars." And so the clapboard edge of colonial architecture shaded by a single elm tree full of health is half a New England village: everything spotless from the shaven grass to the paint and spread of leaves. The bark has the rugate elm-trough look and the leaves take the light as well as did Kipling's new-cut ashlar. The shutters somehow tell you they are green.

This is what Robinson Jeffers meant by "the honey of peace in old poems." And how much better it is, always to wait for the passer-by who never comes than to see him walking forever out of your sight! Everything here is safely out of date and will remain so—far too good for the wrecker's swinging ball; far too old and reverenced not to be good. Charm itself is losing ground in our vocabulary. But charm is an undefinable word. Perhaps it is no more than those tree-shadowed chimneys or the leaf outline against the white. Perhaps it is acceptance.

SUMMER

IN TWO of the fine dunescapes in this book the artist has frozen the swift flight of exactly seven terns. Why seven? Well, if threes and fives are common in botany, as I believe they are, and twos, fours, and fives in biology—as we know they are by simply glancing at a man and a cow—seven is surely one of the magic numbers in the history of man's days on earth. Mythology and astronomy are congenitally happy in the company of seven. There are seven stars in the Pleiades; seven each in Ursa Major and Ursa Minor, for example; and seven principal stars in Orion, of which three form the belt.

Think of the seven hills of Rome; of Seven against Thebes; and recall that in "The Blessed Damozel" ". . . the stars in her hair were seven." Of Homer, we remember (with the help of Browning's words) that "seven cities claimed him." In Blake there is that line:

Grown old in love from seven till seven times seven.

And what of Seventh Heaven in *Maud* and elsewhere? "If seven maids with seven mops," said the Walrus, addressing the Carpenter. "Jacob served seven years for Rachel," says Genesis, a book that also speaks of seven years of great plenty and seven more of famine. In Matthew remember the seven loaves and the few little fishes; and in Revelation, the seven churches and the seven Spirits. Return to Salem and the House of Seven Gables. The list never ends.

For what of Seven Keys to Baldpate? of Beerbohm's *Seven Men?* of Seven Up and seven come eleven? The days of the week are seven; and in *Purgatorio* XXX there is that lovely beginning:

Now when those seven of the first Heaven stood still.

Behind the veil of faëry, the Irish make something of it—or at least Synge did, and did it with a brogue:

May seven tears in every week
Touch the hollow of your cheek.

Aldous Huxley was less poetic than that, but close to Edward Lear's animal gastronomy when he speaks in one of his essays of "the well-known Dance of the Seven Stomachs"—which only the eyeless in Gaza could overlook. And as to nonsense: when James Joyce turns the grasshopper into Gracehoper *(Finnegans Wake)* and further, as a parody on that, into *grausssssss! Opr!*, the mystic seven returns once more in *exactly* seven sibilants, which he might have called (but didn't) the seven hisses.

Wherefore, "Seven is a good handy figure in its way," says Thomas Mann; "picturesque, with a savor of the mythical; one might say that it is more filling to the spirit than a dull academic half-dozen." Hence the seven terns.

WINDY SHORE

FOREST GLADE

ONCE when I stopped to think how many of man's inventions resemble, imitate, and operate like nature's stable and ingenious biomechanisms, I wrote a poem about it. Into the poem I introduced the pitcher plant as a booby trap; snapdragon as a hair-trigger gun; the propellor principle of all samaras—especially the maple seed; the parachute quality of other aerial seeds—the milkweed in particular. I might have continued to include the geometry of spider webs, the ball and socket as in sheddable leaf stems, the crossbill's scissors in the tamarack, the bola spider twirling his weighted weapon, and so on.

Here, though it doesn't actually revolve, and its spokes are sharp, we see what the journeying woodsman often has to circumvent: the perfect structure of the turnstile. The tail of the pheasant etched in shadow points it out. What a remarkable study in all sorts of laterals, for that matter, the artist here achieves.

SOMETIMES, with a thick cloud cover such as this, especially beside the sea, it seems as if a wedge were driven just between it and the far horizon. One looks out toward the light, the magic lifting, as though a giant curtain on the stage were rising, and a world beyond disaster, disappointment, and dismay would open with new promises, new hope. The sea, if so the rising is at sea, lies dark as here, sometimes with these young whitecaps which relieve this cool, calm study. I may be wrong, but usually that curtain never falls. Up, up it goes above us till it lifts to zenith and begins to roll, as here it surely did, into the west. Come night, the stars will be as bright as man could ask. But for intensity of joy I like it best when just one finger will slip under. So it was once, out by Thatchers when there were twin lights, at a time I lost myself in Swinburne. Here we have rocks. But it would be no different ever—would it?—

at the sea-down's edge, between windward and lee.

STRAITSMOUTH LIGHT

THIS SEEMS the moment for a word much overused—exiled today by most of us concerned with language and with poetry. But here we have old trees, a gracious house, a sense of comeliness come and gone, love within and *for* the four old walls: the love Sassoon once spoke of in a poem. Passages in letters from South Berwick come to mind, or words Miss Jewett put inside her books. And yet I turn instinctively to *Perseus in the Wind* by Freya Stark for what I want.

I remember the very day so long ago when one Colonial New England house became, in the instant that I passed it, "the flash of an opening window into depths upon depths of light." The stylist, the great traveller in Syria and Arabia who has "the capacity of Doughty himself," is not speaking here of houses or New England. She is speaking of beauty— and I have used the word. She says of it to wake us:

"The time will come when we shall understand that beauty is no farmyard animal to be fattened at a manger, subservient to a price. One cannot make people live in ugly sites, and turn on culture in a museum, and think it will work. In the *Iliad*, the anger of Achilles is *terrible as the morning star:* this is beauty indeed: the young lover sees it with fear and rapture, dawning in the eyes of his beloved, *'terrible as an army with banners.'* Such is all beauty—a pleasure and a pain, the flash of an opening window into depths upon depths of light, a revelation of awe. But awe is not taught in our schools: economic men have forgotten that these are gods that we harness, though science cannot tell whence they come or what they are, and Socrates by the Ilyssus knew as much as we."

SUMMER SHADOWS

DENDROLOGY has many votaries. Any artist, in his effort and desire to show the nature of a tree, will sometimes etch a single leaf or so in such detachment and clear focus above a wash of leaves, that you know it, without hesitation, for a maple, beech, or oak. With conifers, however, there is just no chance to show the needle cluster, be it two or three or five. But here the combing over all from branch to branch is so astonishingly skillful that one *feels* the texture of the five blades of white pine as well as if one rolled them up and down between the thumb and fingers.

Well sun-sifted too, they give great pleasure in variety of mass. Fragrance is a word, I think, not often critically applied to studies black-and-white—especially of trees. But this grove needs the nose as well as eyes. Or don't you smell the resin?

QUIET GROVE

THE CHOICE of three imposing owls for this collection, plus a somewhat neutral bird who—owls are never *which*—must function as an accent, suggested that the famous small quintet just opposite should be omitted. In the end that seemed impossible.

Mr. Russell Peterson, in his engaging book called *Another View of the City* (McGraw-Hill, 1967), speaks of a hootenanny of six great horned owls one night near his house. I don't know what this would be like, for I have never seen but two owls at one time.

Once in the deep woods of Maine I spotted a baby great horned owl on the low branch of a tree beside the trail between a lake and a trout stream which two friends and two guides and I were following, single file. I brought up the rear. I considered taking him with my landing net, for I had always wanted an owl for the fun of raising him. Later I would give him to a children's museum where he would be safe, admired, and quite possibly happy. But as I reached for my net, the mother—sixty feet above me, and the largest and most angry owl I have ever seen—snapped her beak with the sound of a Paul Bunyan sinking his axe into a Douglas fir. And knowing that such a bird could drop on a mouse like a bullet in feathers, and just as easily slash an artery in my arm or neck, I decided that the *status quo* was the right thing after all. Coming back along that trail in the late evening, the mother hooted at our party from a distant tree. The youngster was not in sight, but the hoot referred to him. That was years ago. Still, if his luck has held, and continues to hold, he will outlive me.

FOG BELL

DOWNY WOODPECKERS

JUST as the Italian *pipistrella* is, without argument, a prettier name than *bat*, so is Quebec's *pique-bois* preferable to me (to my ear, that is) if my other choice is *woodpecker*. How is it with you? And though *sapsucker* has no better claim on music as a word, I must confess to a reason of my own for liking it. For me it means one *particular* bird.

One day, about my fourteenth year and the second of three (no school) on my uncle's ranch in the south of Oregon, I was off somewhere by myself with a .22 rifle in my hand. I had stopped near a giant spruce or fir and stood motionless to watch a red-breasted sapsucker (*Sphyrapicus ruber*) at his rhythmic work five feet above the ground. His eye, I guess, was all for me, and so I was at fault. For suddenly a mammoth red-tailed hawk from nowhere dropped straight at him. I shouted just the barest second before the open talons struck. At any rate, some secondary feathers floated lazily down in answer to my Remington repeater.

Meanwhile the frightened little bird had risen from the ground and pinned himself against his tree. His head moved back and forth as if he were in business, but it was in fact a reflex motion plain as day: the sharp little bill never once touched the bark. He was hammering the air from fright. We eyed each other, just the two of us, and I am sure he understood—not that I had got him off his guard and into danger, but that I had pulled him out of it. At any other time he would have fled the simple sight of me, let alone the four or five-fold crack of one boy's rifle. I knew that I would never again feel so close to a wild bird—so close in terms of his acceptance—as I did that morning in one frozen instant of reward.

A gun was in the hand of each of us in such wild country; but I was beginning to understand its implications. It was a killer, even as the hawk, of the defenseless. That was, or very nearly was, the last time I ever shot at anything alive.

THE THIRD of Mr. Eliot's *Four Quartets*, "The Dry Salvages," which rhymes (he tells you) with *assuages*, opens with a passage referring, fairly obviously, to the Mississippi of his boyhood and with a statement about the river god which surely alludes to a sentence at the close of one of Conrad's best-known novels. Part IV of the V-Part poem is addressed, one may assume, to a statue of the Virgin Mary. There is no such shrine in the compass of the view we are considering, but Part IV of the poem, as well as the lithograph, has a certain relevance to "those / Whose business has to do with fish." It is a very touching passage, even in isolation, and one reader who once sailed across Ipswich Bay on a starry summer night, when *The Waste Land* was a spry young book, is apt to think of it whenever Cape Ann is on his road map of expected landfalls.

Lady, whose shrine stands on the promontory,
Pray for all those who are in ships, those
Whose business has to do with fish, and
Those concerned with every lawful traffic
And those who conduct them.

Repeat a prayer also on behalf of
Women who have seen their sons or husbands
Setting forth, and not returning:
Figlia del tuo figlio,
Queen of Heaven.

Also pray for those who were in ships, and
Ended their voyage on the sand, in the sea's lips
Or in the dark throat which will not reject them
Or wherever cannot reach them the sound of the sea bell's
Perpetual angelus.

MAINE TAPESTRY

THE CORWIN HOUSE

A PERIOD HOUSE by the sea, artfully made; a shade in need of paint; what looks like a rebuilt chimney; a flag proclaiming statehood but for forty-eight; a fitful breeze in the face of a weather-breeding sky; most likely a house with occupants from some fresh level of society: this is an American likeness as inexchangeable for its English counterpart as Whitman of Paumanok for Tennyson of Aldworth. It is the kind of a house in which one could read Mr. Auden's *The Dyer's Hand*—a remarkable and remarkably honest book—much better than I could read again, in a lakeside house not too unlike it, the whole of Lewis and Clark.

Does one ever think of houses in terms of books? I often do; and could easily play the game of just what books from my library I should want at the address of every dwelling in every picture I have ever seen. My copy of Henry Beston's *The Outermost House* is inscribed to the innermost man. This is what I look for in art: what is there in this for me? As Harold Ross of *The New Yorker* used to say in choosing a cartoon: "Where am I in this picture?"

ALL VIEWS of the stable earth, the sea, the mountains, plains, the forest, as the artist takes them in and sets them down, are moments in perpetual suspense. The cryogenic bird in flight, thus frozen, sometimes troubles me the way some mighty comber, showing foam along its ridge, can never break in thunder just when gravity and wind and tide would break it, since it has but one dimension on the canvas or the paper, and is static, not kinetic. But here is something different—a caesura of conviction— which the doe and fawn impart. "Two look at two," as Robert Frost once said. Two look at one, at any rate; and one may look at two and feel that here, for a change, suspended motion is *exactly* right. Italics fit the language of suspension. And so I mean *exactly* right.

THE WOODS

THE OWL is surely one of the best known birds in the world. He is not common and does not multiply like the crow, gull, pigeon, sparrow, starling, grackle, duck, and jay. He hides by day; and yet he is celebrated throughout art, literature, and myth, as the crow, gull, pigeon, and the others are not. Millions in the cities have never seen him in the flesh and feathers. These victims of a doubtful civilization would not even know that dunlin, rail, and ouzel are the names of birds; and yet the pensive figure and nocturnal habits of the owl are as familiar to them as the sight of a dog on a leash on Fifth Avenue or the Champs Elysées. His origin goes back some sixty million years, and one or more of his variant shapes and sizes under perhaps thirty species headings are scattered round the earth, with the exception of Antarctica and a few oceanic islands. Myth has endowed him with wisdom; night with incredible sight and sound equipment. If you want to find an owl in your woods, like this one opposite, wait until you hear the violent clamor of his enemy, the crow. Crows will have found him before you.

GREAT HORNED OWL

PATH BY THE SEA

No THROUGHWAY ever cut by man across the wilderness will give me the compassionate, strange pleasure of his sandy little roads that dip and rise with unexpected curves along the margin of the sea. We do not look for sudden vistas of great sandy beaches, but for smaller ones; for rocky coves and caves; for minor thunder of unangry waters; for the slack and slippery washing of flat tidal ledges; for all those hidden minute laboratories of the ocean that were dear to Rachel Carson. Some of these lie waiting for low water and inspection out beside the promontory now in creamy flood. So many people are beholden to this rare and gifted scientist and poet that her words deserve our summer seascape more than any other.

"There is a common thread that links these scenes and memories [she wrote]—the spectacle of life in all its varied manifestations as it has appeared, evolved, and sometimes died out. Underlying the beauty of the spectacle there is meaning and significance. It is the elusiveness of that meaning that haunts us, that sends us again and again into the natural world where the key to the riddle is hidden. It sends us back to the edge of the sea, where the drama of life played its first scene on earth and perhaps even its prelude; where the forces of evolution are at work today, as they have been since the appearance of what we know as life; and where the spectacle of living creatures faced by the cosmic realities of their world is crystal clear."

ALL THINGS out of their element—even Ariel in *The Tempest*—lose in grace and mystery: the luna moth subtracted from her passage through the night, the landed trout but a speckled scimitar of gleam in the mesh of the fisherman's net, the shot and crumpled hawk in the field, the beached and helpless whale, the ship cradled out of her thrust in the tide and out of remembrance of the fog and gentle groundswell. What strikes us here, however, is the loom of contrast between the craftsmanship of the builder of wooden vessels and the journeyman work in patched old buildings and in rough-plank wharf. The difference between holystone and the adz; between work done with affection and work done for the dollar.

Unlike the moth, trout, hawk, and whale, there is life in the hull before us and water in the harbor aft of her. There will be another launch, another wedding, another voyage, another round of halcyon days, trade winds, thick weather, stormy seas, and ports of call. There will be no fanfare, no champagne; but a ship is always a ship so long as she has a helm to answer to. Pride in a vessel has nothing to do with tonnage, beam, and knots. If you have read *The Shipbuilders* by George Blake, my now departed Clydeside friend and novelist, whose knowledge of his native Scotland was far deeper than Loch Ness, you know what it is when a great ship takes the water. When Mr. Wengenroth's fine book goes down the ways I trust it will have the grace of these sheer bows. For books, like ships, await their element; and the builders as well as the owners have their anxious moments safe on shore.

HOME PORT

STOW WENGENROTH'S NEW ENGLAND

The lithographs in this book, with Mr. Wengenroth's
original titles, except for two which are privately owned,
are part of the Wiggin Collection of the Boston Public Library
and are reproduced with the Library's permission.

The design and typography are by Klaus Gemming, New Haven,
Connecticut, with composition by Finn Typographic Service, Inc.,
Stamford, Connecticut. The printing is by the Meriden Gravure
Company, Meriden, Connecticut, on Mohawk Superfine Softwhite
paper with an eggshell finish. The binding is by the
Russell-Rutter Company, Inc., New York City.

BARRE PUBLISHERS